Service

JESSIE PENN-LEWIS

Power
for Service

A collection of small booklets
dealing with this theme.

Jessie Penn-Lewis

Christian • Literature • Crusade
Fort Washington, Pennsylvania 19034

CHRISTIAN LITERATURE CRUSADE

U.S.A.
P.O. Box 1449, Fort Washington, PA 19034

GREAT BRITAIN
51 The Dean, Alresford, Hants., SO24 9BJ

AUSTRALIA
P.O. Box 419M, Manunda, QLD 4870

NEW ZEALAND
10 MacArthur Street, Feilding

ISBN 0-87508-732-9

PRINTED IN THE UNITED STATES OF AMERICA

CONTENTS

CHAPTER 1

POWER TO WITNESS

"YE shall receive power when the Holy Spirit is come upon you; and ye shall be My witnesses" (Acts 1:8, R.V.). The A.V. margin reads: "When the power of the Holy Ghost is coming upon you," which places the emphasis clearly upon the Holy Spirit Himself rather than upon the "power." The A.V. reads: "And ye shall be witnesses unto Me." "My witnesses," "witnesses unto Me"—both renderings emphasize the personal, living Lord and His work as the purpose of the Pentecostal enduement of power.

The Lord had foreshadowed this in His farewell discourse. "The Spirit of Truth which proceeds from the Father" ("eternally and continuously proceeding," the late Dr. John Smith once pointed out at Keswick), "He shall bear witness of *Me*; and ye also bear witness, because ye have been with Me from the beginning" (John 15:26–27). They had been eyewitnesses of His life, His works, His death, His resurrection, but to make this personal knowledge of His walk on earth effectual they would need the co-witness of the Divine Spirit to His power and glory as the ascended Lord in heaven.

The purpose and the power of Pentecost may therefore be compressed into the few words "*power* to witness." We have often referred to the distinction in the Greek between the words rendered "power" in English, one meaning *authority* and the other meaning *ability*—"dunamis." "Power to witness" has the latter meaning. Not authority to witness, but *ability*. It is the same word used of the resurrection of Christ. "He lives by the *power*—ability, energy—of God"; "Declared to be the Son of God with *power*."

"Power to witness," therefore, means a divine equipping to witness: a divine energy—nothing less than God Himself in the Person of the Holy Spirit coming upon a believer to enable him to witness *effectively* to an unseen yet living Christ, so that the hearer is made to know the *fact* of His death and resurrection and ascension as effectually as if he had also been an eyewitness to these stupendous events—as the disciples were! This divine witness given to the believer is infinitely more convincing than a mental conviction based upon mental reasoning or conclusions based upon evidence, however sound and true. This divine witness makes the unseen Lord a living, present reality to the believer—a Person known and obeyed and loved as truly as the disciples knew and loved Him when He walked the earth as man. "Christian evidences" based upon historical facts are of great value, but they may be said to be mainly *preliminary* in the sense of "rolling away the stone" intellectually, so as to open the door for the Spirit-given revelation to the heart.

As we look out on the condition of things religiously today, we cannot fail to see that the divine "power to witness" is the great need of the Christian Church; for even in churches where the gospel is truly preached in the letter of the Word, how few there are to whom the unseen Lord is a "living, bright reality." The result is that there is little personal devotion to Him, and still less knowledge of His voice and His personal individual control of the believer's life. So much knowledge about the Lord Jesus, with so little direct and personal communication with Him over every detail of life! So little close walking and talking with Him, but so much running about and questioning of each other over the simplest matters—matters made plain in the Word of God but needing to be made plain again to each obedient heart seeking the face of the Living Lord!

"Power to witness" so that the exalted Christ is revealed as a living Person, acting and working in the world as really as when He walked on earth, is needed today to meet the daring assertions of "deceiving spirits" and "teachings of demons" (1 Timothy 4:1, Weymouth) given through the lips of men, themselves deceived, to their eternal loss.

THE SPIRIT OF ERROR

"'Christ' today doesn't mean a Person, but the great advance of goodness and good"; "When we magnify Jesus we disregard God"; "The idea that the world is a wreck or in ruin, and can only be saved by a death on a cross, is a lie. Salvation is the change of life within, or character, and cannot come from any cross or other thing outside of us. There is no doom, no ruin, no curse, no hell, no punishment, no Trinity of Persons. It is all an antiquated, exploded delusion. . . ."

These are brief notes from a sermon delivered to a great gathering of united Christian churches in Great Britain. It is all part of an organized scheme of the fallen archangel, Satan, completely and utterly to overthrow, or nullify, or hide, the glorious proclamation of deliverance and victory over sin, the world, the flesh and the devil through the finished work of the God-Man at Calvary. But it is written that "when the enemy shall come in like a flood, the Spirit of the Lord will raise a standard against him," and our God will come and will not keep silence as He sees the sacred blood of the Son of God counted a common thing. "Power to witness" will be restored to living members of Christ's mystical Church at this time, so that the glorified Christ in the midst of His redeemed ones—the golden candlesticks or lampstands—will be manifested to the world as an undeniable reality.

ABILITY TO WITNESS

But reverting to the "power to witness" which so gloriously came upon the primitive Church, we need to ponder a few points which will help us to see clearly what were the characteristics of the equipping of the Spirit upon them. As *preparation* for the "power to witness" to be conferred later on, the reception of the Spirit breathed upon the company in the upper room upon the Resurrection Day bears an important place. Here the risen Lord showed them His hands and side with the marks of His cross and passion. They thus knew Him as the Crucified and Risen One, and here received from Him the Holy Spirit, communicating to them "the new life of the resurrection." Here they had the path of the new life unfolded to them. They were to be representatives of the risen Lord, even as He had represented the Father. Walking in newness of life, sharing the life of the risen Lord, they were to be a "holy priesthood to offer up spiritual sacrifices," and like the priests in the tabernacle of old would be able to declare whether the sin, typified by leprosy, was put away or retained, according to the faith and obedience of the repentant sinner. The Spirit of Christ in them could discern and would assure of forgiveness when saving grace was manifest. All this would be the result of the Spirit being bestowed that Resurrection Day.

But Peter still went fishing, and still found himself "hurt," or grieved, over an apparent lack of confidence in him by the Lord, and still manifested natural curiosity as to the doings of others (John 21:3,17, 21). In brief, although he had received the Holy Spirit in the on-breathing of the risen Lord, the equipment to witness was still needed. It was, therefore, to these very disciples that the Lord said: "Tarry . . . until ye be clothed with power from on high." On the Resurrection Day He had said: "Take ye the Holy Spirit"; and now He says, "Tarry until. . . ." The one stage is preparation for the other. In the one the believer must take; in the other, the Divine Spirit will come in energizing power at the moment which is either (1) a time of need in service, or (2) a time of readiness, which He alone can bring about. In the one, it is "Take the Holy Spirit"; in the other, it is "Ye shall receive the power of the Holy Spirit *coming upon you.*" In the one case it is for character, in the other for service or witnessing (F.B. Meyer).

THE HOLY SPIRIT USES THE WRITTEN WORD

Another very important condition of preparation for the enduement of power is ofttimes overlooked. An experience is sought for, rather than the principles upon which the Divine Spirit will work being carefully studied in order to be obeyed by faith. *The Spirit of God works invariably along the lines of the written Word of God.* If "power to witness" is to be given, He must have men who know the Scriptures so as to equip them to bear witness along the lines of the written Word.

The disciples were prepared for Pentecost not only by the experiences of the Resurrection Day, in the inbreathing of the resurrection life, but by being carefully taught by the risen Lord Himself in the Scriptures. To the two on the road to Emmaus, "beginning from Moses and from all the prophets, He interpreted to them in all the scriptures the *things concerning Himself,*" and to the assembled company later on also He said: "I spoke unto you, while I was yet with you, how that all things must needs be fulfilled which are written in the Law of Moses, and the Prophets, and the Psalms, *concerning Me.* Then opened He their mind that they might understand the scriptures" (Luke 24:27, 44–45). This shows how carefully He had taught them, as far as they could comprehend His teaching, in the written Word.

The result was that the "fuel," so to speak, for the Holy Spirit's use in co-witnessing at Pentecost was already laid, and there were three lines of witnessing converging for the convicting of souls: (1) The witness of the Scriptures; (2) the testimony of the eyewitnesses of the death and resurrection of the God-Man; and (3) the supreme living co-witness of God the Holy Spirit, the author of the Scriptures and the possessor of the men bearing witness under His energizing power.

This preparation of knowledge of the Scriptures has been often overlooked. Workers think if they are given "power to witness" no "preparation" to speak is needed, and that miraculously they will somehow be given divine "messages." It is true that Peter preached his sermon on the Day of Pentecost on the "spur of the moment," as we would say, but his mind and heart had already been filled with the written Word, for the Lord Himself had opened his mind to understand the Scriptures. So the Spirit of God was using what was already prepared in Peter by the teaching of Christ Himself.

This matter is of primary importance for all who are seeking the enduement of power for service. The Spirit of Pentecost has not changed! The pattern of His co-witness with a believer, giving "power to witness," is clearly seen in the Acts of the Apostles. Every "witness" they gave, however brief, was along the line of the Scriptures, in simplicity of language and in calm, coherent sequence of thought. Nothing "jerky" or dim in meaning, nor in broken sentences needing to be put together and interpreted like some mysterious utterance from the oracle of Delphi, but just plain language which could be verified from the written Word by the most ignorant and simplest believer. And every "witness" embodied the gospel as foreshadowed in the Old Testament Scriptures and fulfilled before their eyes. Ye "killed the Prince of Life, whom God raised, . . . whereof we are witnesses. . . . Repent . . ." (Acts 3:15–19). "Jesus Christ . . . ye crucified, . . . whom God raised from the dead" (Acts 4:10). "Jesus, whom ye slew, hanging Him on a tree. Him did God exalt" (Acts 5:30–31). And "*we are witnesses!*" So it ran!

It was so manifestly the word of the Living God that it was said: "And the Word of God increased." It bore fruit. The "power to witness" was given in power to wield the Scriptures and to speak the Word of God with boldness. When they prayed, it was that the exalted Lord would grant unto His "bondservants" to "speak Thy word with boldness." When the angel of the Lord opened prison doors to the undaunted witnesses, the command was, "Go ye, stand and speak . . . all the words of this Life." The trouble to the chief priests was that the disciples "filled Jerusalem with their teaching"—the teaching that the Man of Calvary, slain upon the accursed tree, was a Prince and a Saviour exalted at God's right hand. And again, when the "work" grew, the apostles quickly saw they must not be diverted from "the ministry of the Word."

WHAT THE APOSTLES TESTIFIED TO

In brief, the book of the Acts of the Apostles teems with passages from the Old Testament Scriptures, showing how the Spirit of God gave His co-witness to those He empowered to witness on the simple lines of Scripture alone. Taught though they had been by Christ Himself, they were not left to "witness," so to speak, as they thought best, but they were kept to the safe lines of the written Word. Peter did not even use any of the striking incidents he had seen in the Lord's life to emphasize this witness! He did not testify to his own experience, except in the briefest way; and he certainly did not give a minute account to his spiritual emotions on that wonderful Day of Pentecost. Likewise, months later, he reported to the apostolic council in only the most matter-of-fact way concerning the events in the house of Cornelius: "The Holy Ghost fell on them, even as on us at the beginning." The apostles preached simply the death, resurrection and exaltation of the Lord Jesus, and used the Word of God in so doing. They passed through, so to speak, all extraneous matter, however beautiful, and gave the pith of the gospel—*Calvary!* The resurrection! The ascension! The call to repent! The coming of the Lord!

This is just what is needed today. Believers indwelt by the Holy Spirit, revealing their resurrection union with the risen, ascended Lord, so filled with the written Word that the Eternal Spirit of the Father can come upon them and energize them to "witness" with boldness, so that they wield the "sword of the Spirit" with such effect that men will be pricked to the heart by the two-edged Word, which is "active," and able to divide asunder soul and spirit, piercing joints and marrow, and discerning the thoughts and intents of the heart. A "Pentecost" which will produce such witnesses the Church and the world surely need. Believers who will not preach their own ideas, or even their experiences as a testimony, but the Word of God in the message of Calvary and the resurrection and ascension of the coming Lord, with such power of God upon them that these stupendous facts become facts to all who hear and a mighty energy in their lives.

But, it may be said, all this is concerning the disciples and the Pentecost of the primitive Church. The same principles stand good *now*. Many are living in the dispensation of the Holy Spirit without knowing the power of the Holy Spirit in their lives. And this, indeed, is manifest in the condition of the Church. The Spirit has been given, for Jesus has been glorified; but it is the work of that same Spirit to make real and true to each individual believer all that Calvary means, and all that union with the risen Lord means—yea, and all that Pentecost means in "power to witness" about a living Person to others. If we seek the fullness of the Spirit and there is no "power to witness" effectively about the risen Lord, so that results follow, then we must assume that somewhere we have failed in the conditions necessary for the Holy Spirit's working. It seems to be in the preparation needed—which we have overlooked—and possibly in the conception of our minds as to what the fullness of the Holy Spirit means!

"Power to witness" is stamped upon every page of the apostolic record! Power to speak the Word of God with boldness! All else was subservient to this. The risen Lord had prepared them for Pentecost by opening the Word to them; and the risen Lord can do this again now in those whom He indwells.

A great and primary "preparation" for the enduement of power for service is being *filled with the Word of God*, so that the Divine Spirit may afterward use the inwrought Word in "power to witness" to all who need the Saviour.

CHAPTER 2

POWER FROM ON HIGH

Luke 24:49

THERE are two distinct regions of need for the operation of the Holy Spirit in the believer: the one embraces life and character, the other has to do with service. But many people are afraid to seek His power in the latter because of extravagances which have been attributed to "the baptism of the Holy Spirit." There is, clearly, an equipping by the Holy Spirit for witness to Christ which the Church sorely needs and which is plainly set forth in the New Testament, but there is much confusion of mind as to what may be expected as the *result* of the promised gift of "power from on high."

First, let us look at the phrase "baptism of the Holy Spirit." In Matthew 3:11, John 1:33 and Acts 1:5 it is always rendered "with" in the text, but "in" is the R.V. marginal reading. The latter expresses most clearly what it is—baptism "in" rather than "with" the Spirit. By this expression we are shown the difference between what occurred in John

20 and Acts 2. In the upper room on Easter Day the risen Christ breathed upon His disciples and shared with them the new life out of death which He was now living. But to these same disciples He said just before His ascension, forty days later, "Ye shall be immersed in the Holy Spirit not many days hence," and "Ye shall receive power when the Holy Spirit is come upon you; and ye shall be My witnesses . . ." (Acts 1:5, 8).*

Keep this therefore clear in your mind as you think and speak of the baptism *in* (or *with*) the Holy Spirit—it is an immersion *in* the Spirit as an environing element which may be described as the Holy Spirit "upon" the believer (as He came "upon" the Lord Christ in Jordan), he being *already* "born of the Spirit" and indwelt and filled by Him.

This is what happened at Pentecost, for the upper room became, as Dr. A. J. Gordon says, "The Spirit's Baptistry." The disciples who had already received the Holy Spirit on Easter Day were now baptized *in* Him as the house was first filled and they were filled, so that they had the divine power *upon* them

---

* "In regard to the Spirit breathed on the disciples on the Resurrection Day being the power of the new life of the resurrection imparted to them, and the Pentecostal gift being more particularly power for witnessing for Christ . . . this substantially expresses the true relation between the two communications of power of the Spirit. . . ."—*Rev. Andrew Murray*

and became equipped witnesses to the risen and ascended Lord.

All this, as concerning the disciples and what took place at Pentecost, is quite clear, but the application of it today is a matter of much divergence of view, mainly through the view being colored by the personal experience of the believer. Also, *the proportion of truth* is sometimes not kept in mind but certain *aspects* of it are emphasized, elements which bind the seeker to other sides of the truth needed for explaining one's experience. For instance, some say, "I received this 'by faith' years ago, but have been disappointed." This has not occurred in all cases, so there was some knowledge lacking which would have cleared the path and given the experiential equipping which was desired. On the other hand, it is true that to "receive by faith" without clear knowledge of what you are to expect and whether you are fulfilling the conditions for the Holy Spirit's working, will end in disappointment.

That John 20 and Acts 2 describe two distinct stages or aspects of the Holy Spirit's work in the believer is beyond question and is borne out by fact, for we see numbers of believers living Spirit-filled lives of peace and devoted service who are manifestly not equipped with liberty of utterance and power for aggressive witness-bearing. They know the cross in its message of victory over sin as declared in Romans 6, but they are still self-conscious and fearful and timid in service for the Lord and dumb as to witnessing for Him. For these there is yet a further stage of knowledge of the power of the Holy Spirit, and the first step toward it is a conviction of their need and the *certainty* that there is for them individually an equipment for service as effective as the disciples at Pentecost knew. *Not* "another Pentecost"—but an apprehension of the fullness of the Spirit for service which is for them in Christ as truly as it was for the disciples in the early Church.

This is the primary fact which must be held clearly in mind as indisputable if you are to seek from the Spirit of Truth guidance into all the truth concerning this vital matter.

THE QUESTION OF "TARRYING"

The subject of "tarrying" or "waiting for the Spirit" requires careful examination of the Scriptures for our guidance.

In the first place, the text usually relied upon as the warrant for "waiting" for the Spirit is Luke 24:49, "Behold, I send forth the promise of My Father upon you; but tarry ye in the city, until ye be clothed with power from on high" (R.V.). Read in the light of simple, ordinary language, we see here merely instructions to the disciples not to leave Jerusalem until the promised coming of the Holy Spirit had taken place, and from an ordinary standpoint as applied to everyday matters this would say that, the Holy Spirit having come, these directions have no further force.

This is reading the Scriptures *dispensationally*, and unless we do so we shall find ourselves in great confusion, for surely what was said in the Jewish dispensation, i.e., before the dispensation of the Spirit opened, cannot be held to be clear directions for those who live under the Christian dispensation. This holds good also for the Lord's words in Acts 1:4–5; i.e., those He spoke to were in Jerusalem, and He charged them not to depart until the Holy Spirit had come, as He had foretold them.

To us, therefore, in this dispensation of the Spirit, there is no *command* to tarry, for how can we "wait" for what God has already given and which, on His part, He waits for us to receive? After the Holy Spirit *had* come the Apostle said "Receive" (See Acts 2:38, 8:15).

To this point we have examined the Scriptural aspect of "tarrying"—what may be called the objective side. But there is the subjective or experiential side, and from this standpoint there *is* often a "waiting." Not a "waiting" ten days on our knees, in imitation of the disciples waiting for Pentecost, but a waiting while God proceeds to make us instruments fit for the Master's use—a "waiting" which generally follows the transaction of faith in claiming our share in the Pentecostal equipping for service. Not a lazy passive "waiting," doing nothing until we have a "consciousness" of power, but a *waiting on God in our hearts* in quiet trust that in His own way He will equip us to the utmost of our capacity for the fullest usableness in His service according to His will. A "waiting" on God which means keen, alert obedience to every bit of light from God, and a faithful, intense service, right up to the utmost of present opportunity and present measure of power.

"THE PROMISE . . . THROUGH FAITH"

Yet even this aspect of "waiting" may become a danger, for it puts before the believer something in the future which may blind him to the present working of God. The truth is, the safest attitude for every child of God is the one of *taking in bare faith* all that God promises in response to one's need, and then trusting God in childlike faith to work it out in the life in His own way. The "equipment" for witnessing is as truly for each believer as the death of Christ at Calvary and all that it means, as union with Christ in resurrection and the receiving of the gift of the Holy Spirit (John 20). While it is true that faith is not knowledge, there is a knowledge which is an absolute necessity before faith can be exercised, for we cannot take what we do not see or believe for something of which we are ignorant. Thus in each case *the apprehension by the believer governs the measure of experience*, and in each no believer has ever yet fully known its depth. Calvary! Resurrection! Ascension! Pentecost! Each to be apprehended in sequence, and each to be known in *deeper depths of experience* as the soul presses on with God.

All the dealings of the apostles with those who had not received the Holy Spirit, as recorded in the book of the Acts, show that they did not look upon the Lord's command to them in Luke 24:49 as obligatory after the Holy Spirit had come; i.e., Peter did not say to the multitude on the day of Pentecost, "*Tarry* as we have done, and ye shall receive." Nor in Samaria, when Peter and John saw that the converts of Philip had not "received the Holy Spirit" (Acts 8:15–17), did they say "Tarry."

The Apostle Paul does not once bid believers "Tarry," but, showing them their *position towards Calvary*, tells them that they are to "Receive the promise of the Spirit through faith" (Galatians 3). Reading, therefore, in broad outline, the whole teachings of the Gospels, the Acts and the Epistles, we see that the word to us who are living in the dispensation of the Spirit is not "Tarry" but "Receive."

Remember, in our saying this, that the *subjective* side is not being considered now but the *teaching of the Scriptures*—as we seek to "rightly divide the Word of truth." We must be careful never to read the Word in the light of our subjective experience, but rather *test the "experience"* by the Word. Many of us have erred in this way in the past, by taking one text—such as Luke 24:49—and quoting it out of its place in the Scriptures, to the perplexity of many seeking souls who cannot understand why there are so many varying "teachings" on the work of the Holy Spirit and even the message of Calvary. The wrenching of single texts out of their contexts and *using them to fit our subjective experiences* has been the cause of much confusion and apparent contradiction of "teaching" on the themes we refer to.

But are there not many exhortations to "Wait" on the Lord, you say? Yes, but if you take a concordance you will see that nearly all these are in the Psalms and have to do with an inward attitude of patient waiting for Him, and upon Him, in connection with many things. In the New Testament the only "waiting" referred to, except the initial waiting in Jerusalem (Luke 24:49), is waiting for the redemption of the body and waiting for the coming of the Lord—*never once a "wait-*

ing" for the Spirit.

The truth is that the Holy Spirit is waiting for *us*, and any delay in our proving of (1) the finished work of Calvary, (2) the power of the resurrection life, or (3) the equipment for witnessing in the power of the Holy Spirit, is due to the blessed Spirit waiting for the truth to break in upon our minds and our then acting in simple faith upon His Word.

THE PREPARATORY WORK

Granted all this, I must repeat that, experientially, there is as definite an "enduement of power," in response to faith laying hold of the fullness of the Holy Spirit, as there is a definite witness of the Spirit to faith laying hold of the forgiveness of sins as the believer's share in Calvary. Or just as there is a definite deliverance from the power of sin and a definite life-quickening power for victory in response to faith laying hold of Christ's death as the believer's death and Christ's life as his life. For each advance there must be preparation, of course. The sinner must be convicted of sin—this may mean time! The believer must be ready to part with sin—again *time*! Yes—and the believer who knows union with the risen Lord needs to be prepared, as only the Holy Spirit knows how, for the enduement of power—

his share in the Pentecostal equipment for service. This, too, means *time!*

The Holy Spirit is in charge of each redeemed soul. Look to Him, and call Him in as "Paraclete," and He will lead you on to know for yourself the enduement of power, when you, too, shall be "*clothed* with power from on high" and become a Spirit-equipped witness to the risen and ascended Lord.

"ENDUED WITH CAPABILITY"

Let us now look at the word rendered "power" in Luke 24:49. It is the Greek word *dunamis*. The Lexicon gives the meaning as "inherent power"; not so much power put forth as power possessed. It is best expressed by "capability." "I will endue you with power that will make you *capable of doing* what I want you to do." *Dunamis* stands for imparted power, and differs from another word translated "power" in the N.T.—*exousia*, which is delegated power, "authority." We know the word *dunamis* as the word from which we get our word dynamite, and that is why we imagine the power of the Holy Spirit will be like dynamite, having an explosive character, but that is not its meaning. It means power imparted by the Holy Spirit to do whatever God wants you to do, however humble, simple, or unexciting that work may be. This is the power which was imparted to the disciples at Pentecost when they were "clothed with power from on high"; and when helpers were needed to "serve tables" and look after the widows, seven men "full of Holy Spirit" were chosen for this humble work.

"*Put ye on* the Lord Jesus Christ" (Romans 13:14). "All of you who have been immersed into Christ have *clothed* yourselves with Christ" (Galatians 3:27, Weymouth). There is a clothing with the Spirit of Christ which means that the human instrument, with its idiosyncrasies, is put out of sight—people do not think about the man or woman, they only see God. We praise God for His blessed gift of the Indwelling Spirit, but do we know what it is to be thus environed with the Spirit of God as the *sphere* in which we live and move and have our being? A clothing that takes away self-consciousness, a clothing whereby we are covered by the mighty hand of God. This is what happened at Pentecost. God Himself broke forth in convicting power, so that His servants did not need to deal with the souls but they were convicted by the mighty presence of the Holy God.

But before God can entrust His children with "power from on high" there is a *foundation work* to be done in their own lives. "Have you forgotten that all of us, when we were baptized into fellowship with Christ Jesus, were baptized *into fellowship with His death*?" (Romans 6:3, Conybeare). The thought behind that word "into" is of action: you were *taken into* His death. Therefore, says Paul, "*Give* yourselves to God as being restored to life from the dead, and your members to His service. . ." (verse 13). This newness of life, with all your members—hands, feet, tongue, etc.—yielded to His service, is basic and vital. Then comes the new freedom—"for sin *shall not* have the mastery over you"; and the new character—"God be thanked that you, who were once the slaves of sin, obeyed from the heart the teaching whereby you were *molded anew*" (verse 17).

That word "molded" (translated as "form" in the A.V. and R.V.) is the word rendered "print" in John 20:25, where Thomas said, "Except I see the print of the nails. . . ." The metaphor refers to the casting of metals. The death of Christ, says Paul in effect, is as a mold in which you are to be shaped, as metal is melted down and poured into a mold, and then takes the shape of that mold. You are to be transmitted into the mold of Christ's death, so that you come out a new character. If you "obey from the heart" the teaching of Romans 6, you will be "molded anew," there will be a new stamp upon you, a new character—the character of the Lamb. Then there will no longer be such contradiction between our profession and our life, and others will catch a glimpse in us of the Lamb of Calvary.

What are we to look for when God answers our prayers for "power from on high"? It is not given for ourselves, or to gratify our own longing for "experiences"; it is an equipment for God's service, an enduement of "capability" to do whatever God wants us to do.

In Matthew 3:11 and Mark 1:8, two figures are used in relation to this enduement. John the Baptist says: "I immerse you *in water*, but He shall immerse you *in Holy Spirit*" (there is no "the" here in the Greek); the spiritual element is contrasted with the material element of water. In Acts 2:2, we are told of the fulfillment of this promise: "Suddenly out of the heaven a sound as rushing violent breath, and it filled the whole house where they were sitting" (Englishman's Greek N.T.). Here again the Word speaks of this enduing Spirit as an element, for the whole house was filled and they were, as had been promised, "immersed in Spirit."

Is not this where we often miss the blessing? We narrow down the working of the Spirit of God to the small capacity of the believer, instead of recognizing that God has said that not only may His children be "filled" but *environed* by His Spirit—that those who are born of the Spirit and joined to Him, "one spirit" with His beloved Son, shall walk through a world that "lives in the evil one"

carrying about with them their own atmosphere—the very presence of God envelop-
ing them. "It filled all the house where they
were," so that not one or two, but *all*, were
immersed in the Presence of God.

THE RESULTS OF THE ENDUEMENT

"And they were all filled with Holy Spirit
and began to speak with different tongues
[languages] as the Spirit gave them to utter
forth" (verse 4). *They* were given power from
on high *to speak*. This is very wonderful. God
does not take hold of a man to speak *through*
him, as the old Greeks thought their gods
spoke to them through an oracle. God did
not speak through the disciples as a mere
mouthpiece, without their cooperation; but
by His Spirit He gave *them* power to speak
forth His word of Truth. This is illustrated
in verse 14: Peter "lifted up *his* voice" and
said, "Hearken unto *my* words." He appealed
to the prophetic Scriptures. He did not pre-
sume to make himself an oracle, but the
"power from on high" which he had received
had equipped him to proclaim the truth of
God and to apply it to his hearers. Then there
was conviction of sin—they were all "pricked
to the heart" and cried, "What shall we do?"
So we see that in New Testament experience,
the first result was:

(1) *Power of utterance*

This we learn from Acts 2:4; and you will pardon my saying that when God gives a man power of utterance, he does not need copious notes! He will preach the Word of God, not his own wisdom, and all he will need will be, perhaps, a list of texts for reference. Are you willing to be an echo, just to say "Thus says the Lord"? It does not matter in the least what *you* think—the people need to know what *God* thinks. Paul requested prayer in Ephesians 6:19 that "utterance" might be given him. What for? That he might make known the glad tidings of the gospel. And he wrote to Christians in Corinth, "In everything ye are enriched by Him, in all utterance . . ." (1 Corinthians 1:5). "To one is given by the Spirit the *utterance of wisdom*, to another the *utterance of knowledge*," and every gift is "given to each for the profit of all" (1 Corinthians 12:7–8, Conybeare). How we do need this gift for the proclamation of the Word of God!

(2) *Boldness in testimony*

This is the second result of the clothing with power from on high. What a lack of certainty there is in proclaiming the truth of God! Oh that men would speak out boldly! Many talk of the things of God as they talk about the things of the world—there is no boldness, no thrusting forth the Word of

Truth. "When they saw the *boldness* of Peter and John they took note of them, that they had been with Jesus"! You who are preachers, teachers, speakers—do ask God to clothe you with *boldness*, so that when you declare the Word of God you declare it with confidence, as one who has learned it at the feet of Jesus Christ.

(3) *Wisdom*

In Acts 6 we find seven men appointed to attend to *the business* of the church, and their qualification was that they were filled with the Holy Spirit and wisdom.

Do you really believe that the Lord can guide you in the ordinary business of life? He can, but you will need first to lay down your *own* wisdom and take *His*—then He will be "made unto you, wisdom." If the church relied less upon the carnal wisdom of the world it would be better. There is too much turning to businessmen to carry their natural abilities and methods into the church, and surrendering the spiritual to the natural. It is a mistake to use worldly "good business" for the church of God, when God can endue with "capability from on high" for the business side of His work. "Look ye out seven men full of Holy Spirit and wisdom to set over this business." If we did this, there would be fewer blunders made. What right have we to call for carnal help? There are churches organized up to the highest degree of perfection—and with not a spark of the life of God in them.

(4) *Power in daily living*

"Be filled with the Spirit, speaking to yourselves with psalms and hymns and spiritual songs" (Ephesians 5:18–19). God can do such a work in us by His Spirit that all that He commands us to do will come about naturally, and not because we feel we *ought* to do it. To make up your mind to praise God may be good, but it is very much better to be so filled with the Holy Spirit that you cannot help praising! What God wants out of us He will first put in. The secret of power for service is to go to Calvary and get rid of the obstacles to the outflow of the Spirit of God, and then ask God for the new life that will bring forth the new fruit. I often hear of things God's children say and do which must grieve Him—and it seems hopeless to speak to them about it. The best thing is to ask God to put a *new life* and a *new spirit* into them, so that they will not do these things.

If you have a little child and are constantly saying "You must not, you must not," you will soon crush the personality of that child. You need to show him how to have a new life within, so that he will *want* to do what is right. God does not expect to get out of us one thing but what He has put into us! Do let us toil, dear fellow-workers, to lead His children into *a life*, and then let that Life manifest itself through their personalities. God does not want us to be all of the same pattern. He will express Himself through each individual in a different way. Just as there are not two faces alike, so He has not made two of us alike in any way, and we must take care that we do not try to mold ourselves or others after the pattern of any other human being.

(5) *Other results*

There are other results of the clothing with power from on high shown in the Word. There is *faith*. Stephen was "a man full of faith and of the Holy Spirit." Faith is not something we have to work ourselves up to— it is the fruit of the indwelling Spirit of God. There is *strength for testimony*. Paul, filled with power from on high, "mightily convinced the Jews . . . that Jesus was the Christ" (Acts 18:28). You may be utterly weak in yourself, but there comes in the divine strength to enable you to testify to Christ. There is also *"the love of God* shed abroad in our hearts by the Holy Spirit" (Romans 5:5); and power to *wield the "sword of the Spirit"* against the principalities, the powers, the rulers of the darkness of this world. The equipment for service is the equipment for warfare.

Have you caught a glimpse of this "clothing" as something that will be around you as an atmosphere—not only the Holy Spirit within, but the Holy Spirit as your environment—"*clothed* with power from on high"? Have you asked God for this "clothing"? Think of it as "capability," for that is what the word "power," in this case, really means. How many incapable people there are about—but this enduement makes you *capable*. It is imparted power, power imparted to you, to make you capable of utterance, boldness, faith, strength, love—in fact, capable to do God's will in your practical, everyday life.

Do we not need this positive power? Are we willing to part with our "own" power, the natural abilities of our "old Adam" life? To make a clean cut with *ourselves*, and step right out in faith upon God and the power He is wanting to impart? It is a dreadful thing for a man to discover that much of his Christian work has been done in the power of his own natural life—his carnal nature. It is a dreadful thing for people who are naturally "capable" when God breaks up the things they have been relying upon—a natural gift of words, perhaps—but He must deal with that before He can clothe you with His own power.

What a grand thing it would be if we all lost our power to "talk"! There is a "natural" flow of words that hinders the Spirit of God. Half a dozen words from the Book and ten thousand words about it! Will you allow the Lord to take the knife of the cross to this superfluity of words? He can never pour out through us in "rivers of living water" until that is done.

Oh Lord, cut us down, *condense us*, both in speaking and in preaching, so that we may be channels for the Word of Life to those Thou dost send us to.

CHAPTER 3

ILLUMINATED VESSELS

"God, who commanded the light to arise from darkness, has Himself shined in our hearts, that we might be ILLUMINATED with the knowledge of the glory of God . . . but we have this treasure in an earthen vessel" (2 Corinthians 4:6–7, Syriac version).

"THE god of this age has blinded the thoughts of the unbelieving that the *illumination* of the gospel" (2 Corinthians 4:4, margin*) should not dawn upon them, writes the Apostle Paul to the Corinthians. The "illumination" he describes as coming from the knowledge of the glory of God in the face of Jesus Christ. And those who are *illuminated* shine as "*luminaries* in the world" (Philippians 2:15, margin), in the midst of all that is crooked, and perverse, and contrary to God.

"Illuminated vessels," then, the Lord purposes His children to be. Illuminated by beholding as in a mirror the glory of the Lord; and "transformed continually into the same

---

* All unmarked references are from the Revised Version (1881). The letters C.H. indicate Conybeare and Howson's translation of the Pauline Epistles.

likeness," the "glory which shines upon us" is "reflected by us, even as it proceeds from the Lord, the Spirit" (2 Corinthians 3:18, C.H.).

But, continues the apostle, "this treasure is lodged in a body of fragile clay, so that the surpassing might [which accomplishes the work] should be God's, and not my own" (C.H.). An *earthen* vessel, although illuminated! A body of fragile clay, although indwelt by the Lord of glory!

In practical life it is important that the heavenly treasure should be clearly distinguished from the "fragile clay," lest the vessel forget and imagine itself to be a heavenly one.

Alas, sometimes the vessel of clay *does* forget that the heavenly treasure is in an earthen vessel, until the Lord permits the buffetings to come, and then there is a sharp and sorrowful awakening.

Let us note first:

THE EARTHEN VESSEL DESCRIBED

"A body of fragile clay" (2 Corinthians 4:7, C.H.).

"The earthly house of our bodily frame" (2 Corinthians 5:1, margin).

"This corruptible . . . this mortal" (1 Corinthians 15:54).

"*The body of our humiliation*" (Philippians 3:21).

These words describe the earthen vessel as it always will be until the Lord's appearing.

It is "*fragile clay*," and therefore liable to be broken beyond usableness if severely strained beyond its power to bear. Alas, how often God's "vessels unto honor" forget this, and treat the vessel as though it were already of the gold of heaven.

It is the "*earthly house of our bodily frame*," and therefore subject to the laws of God made for all bodily frames until they are "dissolved" and the "house from heaven" is given. Alas, alas, how ignorant we often are of these laws of God, and break them as we would not break the ten commandments given on Sinai.

It is called "*the body of our humiliation*"! We are children of God, "heirs of God, and joint-heirs with Christ"; yet we groan, "longing for the adoption [redemption] which shall ransom our body from its bondage" (Romans 8:23, C.H.). "We groan, longing to be clothed upon with our habitation which is from heaven" (2 Corinthians 5:2), for it is humiliating to be fettered by a body of clay, subject to the limitations of its laws, while in truth a citizen of heaven.

THE EARTHEN VESSEL AND ITS SUFFERINGS

"Pressed out of measure, above strength, insomuch that we despaired even of life" (2 Corinthians 1:8, A.V.).

"Troubled," "Perplexed," "Persecuted," "Cast down" (2 Corinthians 4:8–9, A.V.).

"Weakness," "Fear," "Much trembling" (1 Corinthians 2:3, A.V.).

Here we see the illuminated vessel, manifestly mortal and in humiliation. The Apostle Paul does not attempt to hide that he *felt* the buffetings which came upon him. There is no trace in his letters of unnatural stoicism.

In their early days of the Christ-possessed life, many of God's children have thought that it honored the Lord most to hide their "feelings" under a reserved exterior and a reiterated "Praise the Lord!" But how little we understand the real life of Jesus "manifested in our mortal flesh."

We did not see the *unreality* brought about by the suppressing of our humanity, and how, instead of glorifying the Christ, we were really hiding Him, and repelling others who saw the hardness produced by our unnatural conceptions of His life as manifested in vessels of clay. We would not confess that we were "troubled" or "perplexed," and we grieved over our "fear" and "much trembling," sorrowfully telling ourselves how sadly we had failed in realizing the life we longed to live.

Yet "troubled; perplexed; cast down," writes Paul about himself to the Corinthians. The life of Jesus in the earthen vessel is shown by his faith in the faithfulness of God. He is "hard pressed," it is true, but "*not crushed*"; he is "perplexed," but "*not despairing*"; he is often "smitten down" outwardly, but he is "*not destroyed*"; "as dying," yet, behold, he "*lives*." The outward man is perishing, but the inward man is renewed day by day.

Conybeare remarks that the force of the tenses the apostle uses implies that the state of things he describes was *constantly going on*! Not *one* great test and *one* great victory, followed by a life of deliverance from trial.

Nay, Paul writes, "I, in the midst of life, am *daily* given over to death for the sake of Jesus, that in my dying flesh the *life whereby Jesus conquered death* might show forth its power" (2 Corinthians 4:11, C.H.). How clearly the pattern is given us in these words! Daily the vessel of clay is made to know its weakness so that *daily* the life of Jesus which conquers death might show forth its power.

Again, as regards the service for Christ, "weakness, and fear and much trembling" seems always to be the necessary condition of the vessel for the fullest "demonstration of the Spirit, and power." A trembling vessel energized by the Holy Spirit is the picture before us in the life of Paul, yet many of us have been disposed to think that we know nothing of the life abundant when we tremble in giving the message entrusted to us by the Lord. We have thought that the day would come when we should have great *consciousness* of power, forgetting the object lesson in the Apostle Paul.

THE OUTWARD APPEARANCE OF THE VESSEL

"I Paul . . . in outward appearance, am base among you" (2 Corinthians 10:1, A.V., margin); *"I who am mean . . . and lowly in outward presence"* (C.H.).

"Say they . . . his bodily presence is weak, and his speech contemptible" (2 Corinthians 10:10, A.V.).

God's "illuminating vessels" are not always outwardly beautiful ones! Man thinks so much of outward appearance—of a noble presence, of fluency of speech, of strength of body—but God chooses to do His mightiest work with instruments that are often manifestly weak, base and despised. Moreover, He allows them also to remain "contemptible" in the eyes of others, lest they glory in the instrument and fail to see the power of God.

Hence Paul writes to the Corinthians warning them that no man should "glory in men," and bids them learn "not to think of men above that which is written." Indeed, as regards himself he has found it safest not to speak too freely of himself as he is *"in Christ,"* lest any man should have an exaggerated reverence for him and think more highly of him than they ought to think. He found it best to glory in his *weaknesses*, and say little about "the abundance of the revelations." He was willing to remain in the eyes of others a "contemptible vessel," and to accept the truth that in outward appearance he was "base" in their midst. (See 2 Corinthians 12:5–6.)

It takes real self-effacement to calmly accept the truth about ourselves as we are seen by the eyes of others and not shrink back in sensitive self-consciousness from any service the Master pleases—content to speak only broken words if souls are led to Him; to be lowly in outward appearance if the "beauty of the Lord our God" is thereby seen to be from Him, and no flesh glory in His presence.

THE INDIVIDUALITY OF THE VESSEL

"I have been crucified with Christ . . . Christ lives in me" (Galatians 2:20).

"I know a man in Christ . . . on behalf of such a one will I glory; but on mine own behalf I will not glory, save in my weaknesses" (2 Corinthians 12:2, 5).

These words, and many other passages,

show how clearly Paul recognized the personal individuality of the one indwelt by the risen Lord.

The expressions used in Galatians 2:20 seem a contradiction, and yet they are true. "I have been crucified *together* with Christ" (literal Greek) describes a change at the center of the man which, through fellowship with the death of Christ, brings in a new force of the life of Christ to be manifested through the "me"—the personality of the earthen vessel. Hence the apostle says, "*yet I live.*" As if he would say, "I have died in the Person of the Crucified One. I was nailed to the cross in Him. He now lives in me as His temple. Even so, in my personality I live, for I have all my own individual characteristics and tastes. But the life I now live in the body I live by faith in Him, simply working out that which He works in and through me as the fragile vessel of clay. Of what I am in union with Him, I may glory, but of myself as the earthen vessel, I can only glory in weakness—weakness which is the vehicle for the manifestation of His strength."

In writing to the Corinthians, Paul made the same clear distinction between himself as the earthen vessel and the Lord who was his life. He was able to discern when the Lord gave him commandment and when he was using his own personal judgment. "I give charge, yea not I, but the Lord," he writes. "I have no commandment of the Lord: but I give my judgment," are his words later on, and again, "after my judgment: and I think that I also have the Spirit of God" (1 Corinthians 7:10, 25, 40).

The apostle takes no position of infallibility. He knows when God speaks through him, and then he does not hesitate to say it; but he also frankly explains when he is using his own personal judgment, and only ventures to add that he thinks that the Holy Spirit is in accord.

The manifestation of the life of Christ in earthen vessels is transparent and simple. So "natural," and open, and free. It allows no room for insisting that others should accept all that is said as being "from the Lord," and promotes neither a spirit of bondage nor a fear of exercising the mental powers given to men by God himself.

We need, therefore, to recognize the humanity and individuality of the earthen vessel alongside of the blessed indwelling of the risen Lord. Then we may faithfully declare "thus says the Lord" about all that is written in His Word (*not our view of what the word means*, but the word itself simply as it is written) while humbly saying about all light given personally to the soul: "I *think* also that I have the Spirit of God."

THE CONTINUAL NEED OF THE VESSEL

"I buffet my body, and bring it into bondage: lest by any means, after that I have preached to others, I myself [i.e., as a vessel] should be rejected" (or "fail shamefully of the prize," C.H.) (1 Corinthians 9:27).

These words used by the Apostle Paul about himself show the need for constant watchfulness in the daily walk. It is always possible at any stage of the spiritual life to fail in keeping the earthen vessel in its subordinate place, under the complete control of the Lord the Spirit. "I *buffet* my body," writes the apostle, clearly referring to a conflict with his body to "bring it into bondage" and keep it "temperate in all things," so as not to hinder him from winning the prize of the high calling of God.

There is always a "lest I should be rejected" for each one in the Master's service: always a danger of failing shamefully of the prize: of being "not approved" at the judgment-seat of works, where every man's work will be tried by fire and tested for reward.

There is even now the possibility that we might "frustrate the grace of God" in calling us into His service by making it necessary for Him to alter His purpose concerning His using of us, and put us aside for more pliable and faithful vessels. We may turn from the path of sacrifice; we may fail to be "temperate" in supplying the lawful demands of the bodily frame; or we may sink and yield to the cry of its weakness instead of casting ourselves upon the divine strength.

At all times, the earthen vessel must be subservient to the heavenly life, while avoiding the extreme of asceticism and unduly severe use of the sensitive bodily frame. The child of God must walk carefully and with vigilance, lest in lawful things of life there should creep in the choosing of an easier path at the cost of the heavenly prize.

THE DANGER OF THE EARTHEN VESSEL

"Lest I should be exalted above measure through the abundance of the revelations, there was given to me . . ." (See 2 Corinthians 12:7, A.V.).

Again we will emphasize the fact that Paul the Apostle, filled with the Holy Spirit, uses these words about himself! They show that even *abundance of grace* may be a danger, needing the special guarding of the earthen vessel by the Lord Himself.

Paul tells us how the Lord provided for the danger! He gave him a "stake in the flesh" (verse 7, margin), which kept him broken and humbled. Paul calls it a "messenger of Satan," although given to him by God Himself. To Paul there were no "second causes." It looked like a thing that should be taken away, but when he understood from the Lord

that the stake was necessary to cast him continually upon the strength of Christ, the
apostle cries, "Most gladly, Lord," and at once
rejoices in the will of God.

Spiritual exaltation may be manifested in
our looking down upon others not in our
stage of experience. It may show itself in self-
confidence under the guise of "faith"; a spirit
of judgment and criticism with assumption
of spiritual knowledge beyond others; or a
dogmatic assertion of the truth. How subtle
the snare!

But God is faithful, and will guard His
children who trust in Him. He knows how to
give each abundantly used vessel a "stake"
that will keep it broken at His feet. He knows
how to protect His chosen vessels from the
dangers of their natural temperaments and
make it safe for them to be used of Him. He,
who is the Creator, will measure the "stake"
to the need of the vessel, and teach it the
secret how to abound as well as how to be
abased.

Let us therefore, brethren, beloved of God,
"*offer our bodies a living sacrifice*, holy and
well-pleasing to God," while we wait for the
appearing of the Lord from heaven—

"*Who shall fashion anew the body of our
humiliation, that it may be conformed to the
body of His glory, according to the working
whereby He is able even to subject all things
unto Himself*" (Philippians 3:21).

CHAPTER 4

POWER FOR SERVICE AND WARFARE

*"Elymas the sorcerer. . . withstood them. . . .
Then . . . Paul, filled with the Holy Ghost, . . .
said, O full of all subtilty and all mischief,
thou child of the devil, thou enemy of all righteousness, . . . thou shalt be blind, . . . and
immediately there fell on him a mist and a
darkness . . ."* (Acts 13:8–12).*

PAUL is here dealing with the powers of darkness manifesting themselves through one who was definitely an instrument of Satan, having direct communication with the spirit beings of evil and knowing the various methods of obtaining response from them, for he was a "sorcerer." The attitude of Satan toward the gospel of Christ, and toward men who are faithful witnesses to that gospel, is sharply brought out in this incident of Paul's ministry. The Proconsul in Paphos "sought to hear the word of God," but Satan's instrument (Acts 13:6) knew this "hearing" would be fatal to his power over Sergius Paulus, and he "withstood"

---

* See Luke 10:19.

Barnabas and Paul, seeking to turn him aside from the faith. It was then that Paul found a fresh influx of the Holy Spirit rise within his spirit, and "filled with the Holy Spirit" he fearlessly turns to this sorcerer, and fastening his eyes upon him he boldly challenges the Satanic prince of darkness by stripping bare the condition of this instrument, saying, "O full of all guile and all villainy, thou son of the devil. . . ."

The main point of this passage which impresses itself upon us today is the absolute necessity of every child of God knowing what it means to be filled with the Holy Spirit . . . for the purpose of warfare with the powers of darkness. Note again the force of the words: "Then Paul, *filled* with the Holy Spirit, . . . said. . . ." It was the influx or renewed infilling of the Spirit of God into the spirit of Paul that brought about the authority or mastery over the devil and his power in that sorcerer, so that the apostle could say, ". . . thou shalt be . . ." (verse 11) to Satan's instrument, and God bore witness to his words.

It was Paul, in union with the ascended Lord (Ephesians 2:6), *acting from his spirit* as the Holy Spirit moved in him, and he cooperated with the Spirit of God in the exercise of the Lord Christ's authority over the powers of darkness. It was nothing inherent in Paul himself, although he was an apostle. Paul knew this and could distinguish when he spoke as a man and when he spoke and acted specially "filled with the Holy Spirit," as at Paphos. (See Romans 15:18; 1 Corinthians 7:10–12.)

There are many degrees of being filled with the Holy Spirit, many aspects of what that filling means, and many degrees of power in service resulting therefrom. The believer needs to be filled with the Holy Spirit not only for personal sanctification and for preaching the gospel, but for aggressive warfare against the powers of darkness. There is a degree of "filling" which affects only the personal life, and another which means power for service and warfare. This is often termed the "baptism with the Holy Spirit," or the enduement for service, which the Christians of the early Church received on the Day of Pentecost.

To understand the relationship of this fullness of the Spirit to the aggressive warfare against Satan, let us think of the various planes or degrees in the spiritual life. First, there is service on what may be called "the evangelistic plane," when men who are truly regenerated by the Holy Spirit preach the gospel and win souls by the ordinary methods of evangelistic work.

Then there is another plane, which may be called the plane of "revival," where the Spirit of God breaks forth in a floodtide of power, and men are touched, saved, sanctified and filled with the Spirit through a movement of the Spirit of God.

Now this plane of "revival" has particularly to do with the enduement of power for service, and all revivals that have come about through any known instruments have had their rise through those who bear witness to some definite experience, which they may or may not describe as a "baptism of the Spirit"—Finney, for instance, and others who are well known.

Following this plane comes the outworking of the Spirit of God in the believer's life, where he is led into conformity to Christ's death in "the way of the cross." Beyond that, again, lies the plane of "spiritual warfare" which is only understood by the *spiritual* man who has become "spiritual" through the "fullness of the Spirit" and the experiential knowledge of the cross, wherein he becomes crucified to the world and learns to walk after the spirit in the power of the Holy Spirit.

It is very important, therefore, that all who wish to know anything about taking aggressive action against the powers of darkness should be sure that they know the preliminary stages of the spiritual life. They must know what it means to be regenerated by the Spirit of God and have eternal life. They should know—indeed, one may say, *must* know—what it means to be *filled* with the Holy Spirit. They must know the power of the cross of Christ in the meaning of Romans 6, and how to reckon themselves dead to sin and to "let not sin reign," so that they wage war against sin. For it is no use waging war against Satan if you do not wage war against sin. There must be no compromise with or tolerance of any known sin whatsoever in the life; for only while you are waging an uncompromising war against everything in your personal life that would in any way give ground to the enemy, or weaken your victory over him, will you know the power for the spiritual warfare described in Ephesians 6. The question for every child of God in connection with the aggressive warfare against the powers of darkness is: Do you *know* with assurance the fullness of the Holy Ghost, and are you so walking after the Spirit that at any crucial moment such as Paul came to at Paphos when the sorcerer withstood his message, the Spirit of God could move through the organ of *your* spirit in aggressive mastery over all the power of the enemy withstanding the work of God being done through you?

(1) *Is There an Experience for Every Believer Today of an Enduement of the Spirit such as the Disciples Received at Pentecost?*

If that question were put to me, I should reply without any hesitation, "Yes." If you have proved it in your own experience, you have no other answer to give. You have passed beyond the region of debate and theory, and you *know*. Some say the term is not a correct one; but there *is the experience!* In Acts 11:16–17 the Apostle Peter used the words "Ye shall be baptized in the Holy Spirit" in connection with the enduement of power which he and the other men and women received on the Day of Pentecost, and I am at a loss to find other words to use for attempting to make clear to you this crucially important subject.

Before I deal with what this enduement is, and the conditions for knowing it, there are a few points exampled in the Scriptures which it may be well first to note:

(a) It is possible to be baptized into Christ without having received the baptism of the Holy Spirit. Acts 8:16 says that the Samaritan converts had been "baptized into the name of the Lord Jesus" but that the Holy Spirit had "fallen upon none of them."

(b) It is possible to have knowledge of the risen Lord without being filled with the Spirit in the way of enduement for service. This is clear from Paul's experience recorded in Acts 19:1–7.

(c) It is possible to be baptized with the Spirit apart from all *exterior* conditions whatsoever, as exampled by the men in Cornelius' household. See Acts 10:44–48.

The Acts of the Apostles, giving the record of how the Holy Spirit came to the infant Church, has a large number of examples of His varied ways of working in and among men. There is no rigid system laid down by God for His working. The Holy Spirit is a Person and requires certain conditions of cooperation with Him for His working, and He responds to these wherever they are found.

We live in the dispensation of the Holy Spirit, which began when He came on the Day of Pentecost, and therefore *are in the same dispensation* as the days which followed that wonderful day. Paul in his epistles unfolds the work of the Holy Spirit in His building of the Body of Christ; but the Acts of the Apostles shows varied ways in which the Holy Spirit makes Himself known to men. If the converts in Samaria were "baptized into the name of the Lord Jesus" and yet needed to be prayed for "that they might receive the Holy Spirit," there are *multitudes* of converts today in that same condition. There are those who truly know the risen Lord and are fully consecrated to Him, yet they lack that "filling" which Paul afterward received, which enabled him so quickly to proclaim Christ with boldness.

There are also large numbers of God's children today who have definitely received the Holy Spirit as a Person and who do know

Him, but they have no *power for service*. They have fulfilled the conditions for His indwelling by an absolute surrender to God to do His will—in the cleansing of the heart from the love of sin, and in faithful obedience up to light, with the resulting "fruit of the Spirit . . . love, joy, peace." But to them it has meant inward victory and fellowship with God, with very little change in power for aggressive service.

They do not apprehend that "power" is a Person, and that on the ground of their identification with the Lord at Calvary they may count upon the Holy Spirit as the Spirit of Power *as well as* sanctification. We receive Him as a Person who is Power, and He becomes increasingly manifest in energizing power for service as the believer passes on from plane to plane and on to appropriation. Note now:

(2) *Peter's Description of Pentecost and What It Meant.*

"As I began to speak, the Holy Ghost FELL *on them, even as on us at the beginning"* (Acts 11:15).

"Then remembered I the word of the Lord . . . ye shall be baptized with [R.V. margin: IN] *the Holy Ghost"* (Acts 11:16).

On the Day of Pentecost (Acts 2:33), Peter said, "Being by the right hand of God exalted . . . He hath *poured forth* this." Notice the words "poured forth," a "baptism *in*," a "falling *upon*." There are two other verses with the same thought: Acts 1:8, "Ye shall receive power when the Holy Ghost is *come upon you*: and ye shall be My witnesses." These are the Lord's own words. Then in that passage about Samaria: "For as yet He had *fallen upon* none of them"; and Acts 10:45: "On the Gentiles also was *poured out* the gift of the Holy Ghost." These sentences, put together, are a very striking description of what took place at Pentecost. "He has *poured forth* this." "As I began to speak, the Holy Ghost *fell*." Then note:

(3) *The Marked Result of the Pentecostal Enduement.*

> "*They were all filled . . . and* BEGAN TO SPEAK . . ." (Acts 2:4). "*When the Holy Ghost is come upon . . . ye shall be My* WITNESSES . . ." (Acts 1:8).

There is, then, an "enduement of power," or a "baptism of the Spirit," or a "fullness of the Spirit," that means *power of utterance for witness* to a living and ascended Christ: an infilling of Spirit that has to do with service for God rather than with the personal life of fellowship with Him and victory over sin.*

---

* "The fullness of the Spirit is, I think, to be distinguished even from the indwelling of the Spirit; and its

Now what came about experientially in these believers when the Holy Spirit thus "filled" them or "came upon" them? The teaching of other parts of Scripture and the knowledge of experience make it clear. Briefly, it may be said, that the "falling upon" of the Holy Spirit, described by Peter as taking place on the Day of Pentecost, meant an influx of the Spirit of God *into the human spirit* whereby it was released from its imprisonment in the vessel of the soul and lifted into a position of domination over soul and body. Just here arises the crucial question as to

(4) *Where the Holy Spirit Resides in a Believer.* *

> "His Spirit in the inward man" (Ephesians 3:16), *i.e., the regenerate human spirit* (Moule).

So many of God's children do not know that they have a "spirit." They live in the "soul"—that is to say, in their feelings, in their sense life, or in their minds;† but as to what is "spirit," they do not know. Nor can

---

leading characteristic [is] the outgoing of power. . . for service, coming from the Holy Spirit, and permeating the soul (i.e., the personality) . . ." (Dr. Elder Cumming).

* See *The Spirit of Christ* (Note C.) by Dr. Andrew Murray.

† See *Soul and Spirit* for fuller light on this.

they know, until by the Holy Spirit coming into their spirit they become conscious of the existence of their own spirit. "Take ye the Holy Spirit," said the Lord. When you do this, He comes into your *spirit*, for He is the Spirit, and, as Fausset says, "The spirit is the recipient of the Holy Spirit" and is "the organ of the Holy Spirit." The Lord said, "God is Spirit, and they that worship Him must worship" not in soul but "*in spirit . . .*" (John 4:24).

Until a Christian receives the Holy Spirit as a Person, although he may be regenerated and "born of the Spirit," his Christian life is more mental than spiritual. He may be out-and-out loyal to Christ, but it is mainly in the realm of the will and of the mind. Then a great change takes place when he is brought to receive the Holy Spirit, and he becomes conscious of a life after the spirit (i.e., in the realm of the spirit) in more or less degree.

But a still greater change takes place when, by the teaching of the indwelling Spirit, the believer sees that there is yet for him a fullness of the Spirit for *service*, which will enable him to be an effective *witness* to the risen Lord and equip him for *aggressive warfare* against the powers of darkness.

The distinction between these two aspects of the fullness of the Spirit has been clear in my personal experience, and I can now see what this enduement wrought for my spirit as well as my mind and body.

I was reading Andrew Murray's *The Spirit of Christ*, and as I read I saw that I should know the Holy Spirit as a Person. So I took Him as the gift of Christ, as simply as I at first took the Lord Jesus as my Saviour. I well remember the deep peace, the fellowship with God, the communion of the Holy Spirit, and the fruit of the Spirit in love, joy, peace, which followed. But I could not understand why it made so little difference in my service. It did not deliver me from shrinking inability to speak boldly for Christ, *nor did it give me power for aggressive service.* In these respects I was just the same as before, until, some three years later, I saw that there was a fullness of the Spirit for *service*, which meant deliverance from the fear of man and power for effective utterance in witness for Christ.

When that enduement of power came to me, it was truly an influx of the Holy Spirit which can be described as a "falling upon," for my spirit was suddenly released from every bond and seemed to break through into the heavens as from some inward prison, finding its place in the very heart of God. It is difficult to find words to describe spiritual things, but as clearly as I can express it, these words define what happened. Then, manward, through the organ of my freed spirit, poured forth *through my mind and lips*, with ease and boldness, the message of God from the Scripture, illuminated with the very light of heaven. The result was deep *conviction of sin* on the part of the hearers and wondrous blessing from God.

The enduement of power is, therefore, very clear to me as a greater influx of the Holy Spirit into a spirit already indwelt by Him. It can be described as a "coming upon" the human spirit in such a measure as to clothe it with light and lift it out of what Tertullian and other writers have called the "vessel of the soul," which is as a dark film around the spirit until it is thus set free.

It is *not* a "coming upon" the soul or body, because the Spirit of God is *spirit* and He fills and clothes the *spirit*, and raises the *spirit* into freedom. He comes into your life from and through the channel of your spirit within you, illuminating the mind and setting free your faculties for the service of God.

(5) *The Baptism of the Spirit May Be Followed by Many Fresh Infillings of the Spirit.*

It is clear from examples in the Acts of the Apostles that a special influx of the Spirit of God may, after the first liberation of the spirit, occur again and again as need may arise, if the believer knows how to walk after the spirit and how to fulfill the laws of the

spirit for cooperation with the Spirit of God.
It was just such a fresh influx of the Holy
Spirit which broke forth through Paul in
dealing with Elymas, and which meant victory over the devil in that sorcerer. It was
this fresh infilling which arose in the spirit
of Peter when it is said of him, "Then Peter,
filled with the Holy Ghost, said . . ." (Acts
4:8); and when Paul, being "troubled," suddenly turned around and commanded the
evil spirit to leave the girl at Philippi (Acts
16:18).

For this, the believer must know how to
live with a freed spirit. Through ignorance
of the laws of the spirit life, the spirit may be
allowed to sink into the vessel of the soul
again, as if it were in prison, and thus become out of cooperation with the Holy Spirit
in effectual service. If I am walking in the
spirit and meet such a one, my spirit seems
to beat against that "soul wall" as I speak to
that person, and I say, "I cannot find touch
with your spirit." When the spirit sinks into
the vessel of the soul, the believer sees everything from the "natural" standpoint. It is
as if a thick film has enwrapped the spirit;
things around become subject to the inter-
pretations of the natural or earthly mind,
while God's viewpoint is obscured. If a fresh
influx of the Holy Spirit came again into that
one's spirit and lifted it to its right place of
dominance, he would see all things from the

spiritual standpoint; for the spirit is again open to the Holy Spirit as His "organ" or channel, and "liberty of the spirit" with power of utterance is again given for any special service. These are the moments when the face is radiant and the heart is filled with the love of God (Romans 5:5).

This liberation of the spirit is what takes place in meetings where the Spirit of God is manifestly present, but believers should know how to "walk after the spirit" *every day*, and understand the laws of the spirit so as to keep the spirit always free for coaction with the Spirit of God and open to His monitions.

It is because of the sinking down of the spirit into the soul vessel that believers lose what they call the "experience" of the enduement of power. They need to be taught what causes this sinking down, and why they lose coaction with the Spirit of God and walk again "as men" (1 Corinthians 3:3, A.V.)— that is, like ordinary men, rather than men ruled and governed by the Spirit of God.

(6) *The Baptism of the Spirit and the Mind.*

It is very important to understand that the influx of the Spirit of God into the believer's spirit invariably illuminates the mind, which is renewed and filled with light—even the light of the Spirit of God. Then the spirit will be free, and the tongue liberated to witness as the disciples did on the day of Pentecost. They were "all filled," and as the Spirit of God clothed each spirit, the light flooded their minds and they began to talk about the wonderful works of God. The illumination of the mind is most marked in Peter. He had been taught by Christ, and consequently, under the power of the Holy Spirit, when he heard the men outside mocking, he rose and gave a wonderful picture of Christ as revealed in the Old Testament prophecies. Scripture was illuminated. He could put together, on the moment, the promises of the Psalms and what David foretold about Christ so that his Jewish hearers could not deny them. He was enabled to use the Scriptures in order to convince his hearers that "Jesus" definitely was the Christ. The Holy Spirit coming into his spirit illuminated his mind and gave freedom of utterance to his tongue, with the conviction of the Holy Spirit behind his words. But it was Peter *himself* who spoke, by the energizing power of the Spirit of God.

How different this is to the idea that to be "filled with the Holy Spirit" you must *not use your mind*, and that when He fills a believer He uses his tongue like an automaton. It is not so with Peter, for there we find the illumination of the mind, the flood of light upon the Scriptures, and the intelligent utterance of what he had grasped and knew by the enlightening of God. The misconception that the use of the mind is a hindrance to the manifestation of the Spirit opens the door to Satan's counterfeits of the working of the Holy Spirit. If a believer thinks that when he speaks "as the Spirit gives utterance" he must merely open his mouth and let some supernatural power use his tongue, while his mind is a "blank," he is fulfilling the formula for becoming a medium for evil spirits. A man who desires to become a spiritualistic medium understands that any *action of the mind* breaks the supernatural power he wishes to take possession of him; whereas the full use of the mind is coexistent with the true working of the Holy Spirit.

The *action or non-action of the mind* is a primary distinction between the true working of the Spirit of God and the counterfeit working of deceiving spirits, and if God's children do not know how to discern the true and the false on this primary ground, they cannot tell the true from the counterfeit in Satan's deceptive workings today.

The mind of Peter was in full action on the Day of Pentecost, and it is manifest that he was perfectly intelligent and conscious of what he said and did, for he was capable of standing up at once and seizing the opportunity of speaking to the mockers among the people. I am emphasizing this because the true fullness of the Holy Spirit must not be lost for fear of counterfeits. You should seek to understand the laws which govern both so that you may discern and enter into all that God has for you.

(7) *The Baptism of the Spirit in Its Results Godwards.*

It is very striking to find, in going through the chapters in the Acts, that all the early believers talked about *Christ risen and ascended to the throne in heaven*, but very little is said about personal *inward* experience. There is hardly a trace of it. They did not preach what they had obtained inwardly, but proclaimed a glorified Christ on the throne.

This shows that a true baptism of the Holy Spirit does not turn the recipient *inward* to himself, to cultivate some personal experience and have a good time, but turns him Godward and manward. The Christ they talked about was a *Christ in heaven.* Peter said: "He, being by the right hand of God exalted, has poured forth this . . ." (Acts 2:33).

This is fully in harmony with the Lord's words on the eve of His cross when He said, "At that day ye shall know . . . ye are in Me, and I in you," which briefly means that when you are worshiping the Christ in heaven, by the working of the Holy Spirit dwelling in your spirit, Christ is revealed as a living reality; but you are not to turn *inward* to worship Him. That is, the "*I in you*" is *the result* of the "*ye in Me*" in spirit, joined to the risen Lord in heaven; and as you keep open towards Him, He shines in you and is revealed to others. As soon as *you turn inside* you practically turn from the light of His glorious face into darkness. The "Christ in you" is the *effect* in you, caused by the Spirit, of your attitude towards the Christ upon the throne.

Crudely put, it as though you look out at the sun and the sun shines in—then others see the sunlight there; but as soon as *you* turn away from the sun to look within, it is darkness. While you are occupied with Christ upon the throne, worshiping Him, and your spirit is open to Him, the Holy Spirit is revealing the Christ within and supplying to you the "Spirit of Jesus" (Philippians 1:19). God never meant that you should set up a special "altar" in your heart where you are to worship. *Christ is in heaven*, and we as members of His Body all come to worship one Christ and are all "made to drink of one Spirit," which He pours out from Himself to all the members of the Body as they are holding, and looking toward, Him as the Head. A further result is that

(8) *The Baptism of the Spirit Is a Baptism into the Body of Christ, and into One Spirit with All Others United to Him.*

> "*In one Spirit were we all baptized into one
> Body, whether Jews or Greeks, whether bond
> or free; and were all made to drink of one
> Spirit*" (1 Corinthians 12:13).

The baptism of the Holy Spirit means an
influx of the Holy Spirit into your spirit which
takes you into unity of spirit with others
drinking of the same Spirit. It is only when
the enemy drives the children of God down
out of the spirit sphere into the vessel of the
soul that they become, as it were, shut up
into "separate compartments," possibly occupied with some inward experience and
wholly forgetting the unity of the Body of
Christ.

John the Apostle wrote, "If we 'walk in the
light' as God is in the light, we have *fellowship one with another. . . .*" It is difficult to
find language to express these facts in the
spiritual sphere, and it is crudely put when
I say that as soon as a believer turns to an
inward "experience" from worship and fellowship with God in heaven, he turns *down*
into the dark vessel of "himself" and loses
the fellowship which he had in the spirit
sphere of light, with all other members of
the spiritual Body of Christ. The forces of
darkness rejoice to see a believer turn into
himself, for they know well that thus he turns
from the inflow of the Spirit of God, which
circulates freely from spirit to spirit in the
members of the Body of Christ as they "hold

the Head" (see Colossians 2:19 and Ephesians 4:15-16) and "*grow up . . . into Him,*" and not down into the self-center of themselves.

(9) *Why Believers Lose the Joy and Liberty of the Baptism of the Spirit.*

The main reason is that so few clearly understand the laws of the spirit for retaining a liberated spirit in cooperation with the Holy Spirit.

Let us suppose a believer receives the baptism of the Spirit, and finds his spirit free and filled with light, buoyancy, joy and liberty. But before long something goes wrong in that one's daily life, and a shadow comes on his spirit. He does not know what has caused the shadow, and perhaps is hardly conscious of it, so it is left there. Something else happens later on—again, another little shadow on the spirit which is undealt with. Meanwhile, the powers of darkness are watching. They say, "We must stop this man. He will do some mischief to our kingdom if he goes on and the Holy Spirit is able to work unhindered through his spirit." So they watch and gather around, and *put the pressure on.* Presently, through outward things— perhaps opposition, antagonism, criticism, with slowly increasing shadows, clouds, weights and troubles—the powers of darkness come down on the spirit and push it slowly down, down, down into the soul, until it sinks right in, and the buoyancy of spirit and light and liberty seem gone.

Now the believer goes to his knees and tries to get the "experience" all over again. In his struggle to regain what he *thinks* he has lost, he turns more and more inward, more and more down into the "soul"—or in other words, into himself—instead of out toward the light, casting off the shadows, weights, clouds which have gathered around his spirit. Perhaps he does not think about the existence of the "hosts of wicked spirits" in the "heavenly places" which have gathered around his spirit to drag or drive it down from the heavenly sphere.

Instead of, by faith, fighting through the shadows and maintaining his position with Christ in God (Colossians 3:3), this poor believer cries out for his "experience" again! "Ah," says the enemy, "I will give him an 'experience,'" so he gives him in the *soul realm* a counterfeit of what the believer *knew at first in the spirit.* Now it is in the *body* and in the *sense realm.* Joy, liberty, buoyancy— these he experiences again, with perhaps much more added on—in beautiful pictures to the mind and "feelings" which seem so heavenly.

If the believer does not know what is "spirit" and *what is from his senses,* he opens himself without question to all this "experi-

ence," and cries, "Oh, I have it all back. I
have waited many hours for this. This must
be of God!"

And it *looks* all right, until a little later on
the traces of the enemy's work begin to ap-
pear. This believer, who was once so simple
and childlike, begins to show an unteach-
able spirit; then he gets "infallible" in his
"guidance" and dogmatic in his assertions;
then he loses power to see right from wrong
in matters needing a keen-edged conscience;
and slowly the enemy gains, until some day
the "beautiful" experiences disappear and he
finds he has been deceived by the subtle foe.

(10) *The Danger of Quenching the Spirit.*

But there are others who do *not* "get back"
an "experience." The enemy's working has
been on another line. These are poor
"quenched" souls. Some of them may even
think they have committed the "unpardon-
able sin" and can never get out of the prison
of themselves. They have again turned in-
wards, and are crushed. When you speak of
the "baptism of the Spirit" they look at you
so sadly and say, "Ten years ago I had that,
but I lost it." Or, "Ah, it was only a passing
experience."

What is the matter? They have a
"quenched spirit." What quenched it? Sin?
Nay, *it may not have been so at first.* It was
just some shadow which came purely from

ignorance, but they did not know how to throw the weights off their spirit, and how to keep it in freedom and open and clear for cooperation with the Spirit of God.

In Great Britain alone there are many children of God who once knew a definite, real influx of the Holy Spirit into their spirits, but the outside things, with the powers of darkness behind them, drove the spirit down into the prison of the soul. If these believers were only released in spirit we would have revival in Great Britain.

Child of God, have *you* a *quenched spirit*? You can look back to the moment when you knew you were filled with the Spirit, and then you thought you disobeyed God over something, and the enemy charged you with it. Perhaps he said, "You have grieved the Holy Spirit," so you tried to "get right" and could not. You did not know it was the enemy's accusation, and did not understand how to resist it and cast the shadow of it away from your spirit. You admitted this charge from the enemy, and it brought upon you darkness and disappointment and hopelessness and despair. Then your spirit closed up as in a vice, and now it needs to be liberated and once more made open to the influx of the Spirit of God.

Do not get astray again by turning inward, but lift up your eyes to God and say, "Lord, release my spirit, and make it again a free organ for Thy Spirit to pour through," and then obey God right up to the light you have. You have enough to see what a difference there would be if your spirit was liberated instead of bound, and you can *choose* that God shall do it. The difference between *wanting* to have a thing done and *choosing* to have it done, is vital. You can say, "Lord, I want it." Yes, but do you *choose* that it shall be done? That is to say, do you put your will on God's side that it *shall* be done? For with the full, honest cooperation of the will of a man, God can work. "If ye abide in Me . . . ye shall ask what ye will"—not what ye want, but ye *will*—"and it shall be done."

(11) *Conditions for Receiving the Holy Spirit as a Person.*

These are (1) the putting away of every known sin, and (2) a definite trust in the power of the blood of Christ to cleanse the heart from the love of sin. In other words, a cleansing of the inner spring of the heart life, so that the believer is delivered from the "must" sin *and* the "want to" sin.

You must take heed not to confuse the center with what may take place in your circumference. You may be suddenly beguiled into some act which is visible, conscious sin, but this does not mean that in your innermost being you do not *hate* sin. Keep it clear that in the center spring of your heart life you have been cleansed from the love of sin, and do not now *want* to sin. In brief, lapses into known sin should be exceptions and not the rule. You no longer practice sin as a habit (1 John 3:9).

The third condition for receiving the Holy Spirit as a Person is implicit obedience to light. You must at all cost do what you know to be *right*, up to your light. This means full surrender to do the will of God when you are sure of it.

Let me press these points personally. Have *you* put all known sin out of your life? Have *you* trusted the Spirit of God to cleanse your heart from love of sin? Are *you* surrendered to God, so that you can look up into His face and say, "Lord, You know, without any quali-fication, I *choose* Your will, and will do it as far as I know it"? This is absolute surrender to God. Are you obedient up to all the light you already have, i.e., are you *acting out* all that you know to be right?

This is an important point. The incoming of the Holy Spirit as a Person to dwell in you quickens your conscience, and you must take heed not to quench the voice of con-science. The more you *do* what you know to be right, the more clear and acute will grow the knowledge of what is right and wrong. There is nothing that dulls the working of the Holy Spirit in your conscience so much as to go against what you *know to be right*, as your conscience continually becomes more enlightened by reading the written Word. And so I press the point to all who desire to be filled with the Spirit: "Are you true to the light you have, and obedient to the voice of God in your conscience?"

Set aside, for the moment, the question as to what is the specific will of God for you; stick to the simpler point, at first, of *choosing* between right and wrong. You will get into confusion if you have the thought that to do the will of God He must make known to you whether you should, for instance, go down a certain road. God's will is that you should do *right*. If you think you are to be told by the Holy Spirit every little thing all day long, then you become a mere machine and do not require any intelligent perception at all.

There are occasions when the Holy Spirit through your spirit makes you know the special guidance of God, but for your daily life God guides through your senses of right and wrong, i.e., by your conscience and understanding. Ask about everything "Is this *right*?" and it is astonishing how clean-cut the line will become, and you will soon understand the way the Holy Spirit would have you go.

Finally, by an fact of faith, take the gift of the Holy Spirit. All these conditions you can fulfill with your will. You can take these steps today and stand firm to them as a transaction with God. You can say now: "I *will* to put out of my life every known sin; I *will* to trust God to cleanse my heart from the love of sin; I *will* to be obedient to God right up to the hilt of what I know to be right; I *will* to be fully surrendered to God right up to my knowledge of His will; I *will* to take the Holy Spirit now, by deliberate faith, into my spirit, to fill me and to teach me." And this can stand as a transaction with God from which you must never swerve. This is the receiving of the Holy Spirit.

(12) *Conditions for Receiving the Enduement of Power.*

Those who have received the Holy Spirit as a Person and have even walked in communion with God for some time may yet say, "I have no power for service, and I see that I need a real fullness of the Spirit for definite service." What are the simple steps you take for this? Practically the same as the steps I have already named, but in a fuller degree of appropriation, and with the addition of a full surrender to God *for any possible kind of service He wishes you to do*, without any personal bias.

The first was full surrender to God to do His will in your daily life. Now it is full surrender to God for God to choose the *service* for you. So that if He wishes you to go to the kitchen to serve Him there, you will be as contented with it as if He had said, "Go up to that platform to give My messages."

There are many believers who want a baptism of the Holy Spirit to make them successful; some want it to save them the trouble of reading their Bibles and preparing for a meeting. They say, "It would be delightful to be able to stand up and speak as Peter did," but they forget the preliminary training he had had for three years by the Lord and, after the resurrection, the opening of his understanding to understand the Scriptures.

I received the baptism of the Holy Spirit in so definite a way that it remains as clear to me in its detailed steps as the hour of my conversion. To make it clear to you, I will just go over some points which show the steps that God led me along—first in the reception of the Spirit and then, three years later, in the enduement for service.

(1) Surrender to God, and victory over sin as the result of that consecration. This lasted some years; then came (2) the definite reception of the Holy Spirit as a Person, with the resulting peace, joy, etc. But still no power to witness in aggressive power. Some years later came (3) the *conviction of need* for an enduement of power. For three years before this I tossed over the question, "Is it

possible?" Then I sank under the thought "It is not for believers now." But I could not rest. Back came the cry, "Is there not a fullness of the Spirit that will release me for service?" until I caught sight of it in another, and then I said with assurance, "Now I *know*. What that soul has is what *I* want."

Let me say, before we go one step farther, that to deal effectually with God on this matter, you must come to a deep conviction that there is an enduement of power for *you personally*. You cannot make headway until that is settled. I lost, as I have said, three years over it. I read books on the subject until I was worn out with disappointment, for none seemed to say clearly how this enduement could be obtained. Again I was confused, because some people said there was an "enduement" and others said there was not, and I was torn with questions until there came absolute conviction by just a glimpse in another of what I was after. Then I said, "I will go straight to God and ask Him to *prove* to me whether there is *for me* an enduement for service that will liberate me in utterance as it did Peter at Pentecost. I will put it to the proof for myself." Away went the books, and away went the various views and theories. In desperation I said, "*I will go to God.*" From this time I never admitted another question, but set myself with steady determination to prove for myself if there was anything in it. Then slowly, as I held on to God, there grew within me a deepening purpose, that at all costs I would obtain this enduement for service—until at last there came such a cry to God for it as the supreme thing I wanted that I could say He might take away all things from me if only He would answer this cry! It was a long time before it got to that, but it brought about such an absolute surrender of my will to God that I have never had to fight a battle of "surrender of will" from that time. I was able to say He could do absolutely what He liked with my life, if He would only give to me that liberation of the Holy Spirit that *Peter knew at Pentecost.*

Peter was the pattern I put before the Lord. I saw that Peter was not "nervous" that day, and I intensely felt my great need was to be delivered from an overpowering nervousness and a kind of paralysis in speech that fairly mastered me. I cried, "I want the deliverance that Peter got at Pentecost. I do not care what Christians call it. If 'the baptism of the Spirit' is not the right term, give me the right words to use. I do not care about the words, but *I want the thing.*"

In this way I held on to God with an intensity which caused "people" to fall away from my mind—and all they said about this great liberation for service which I was seeking. Then a deep rest came into me that God would *do* what I had asked, and I could wait His way and time.

Thus I learned the true meaning of "waiting" for the "promise of the Father." I had reached a quiet attitude of dependence upon God, that He would answer my cry in His own time. Then I went on with my usual work, not in indifference, but with a steady hold of faith that at some time the "enduement" would come. But I was sorely tested. My experience after that was a deeper and deeper sense of failure. Everything seemed to be worse and worse instead of better and better, as I thought it would be after such a tremendous and deliberate transaction with God. I appeared to lose all I already had. I grew worse and worse in nervousness and "horror" in speaking to my Bible Class, and everything seemed a failure.

Then came a most awful revelation of the way in which "consecrated self" penetrated my Christian work, in the sense of self-energy. The unveiling was truly a horror to me, and brought me in deep abasement to the blood of Christ for cleansing. It was the precious blood of Christ which did the deep work of cleansing my heart from the love of sin when I received the Holy Spirit as a Person, but now Romans 6:6–11 became a power to me, and I knew the meaning of "our old man was crucified with Him . . ." and what Paul meant by his words "crucified with Christ" (Galatians 2:20).

After this there was a pause, and for weeks and weeks I left the matter with God. It was settled with Him, and He was just to answer my cry in His own way. Then two or three searching questions were distinctly put to me by the Spirit of God. The first was: "If I answer your cry, are you willing to be unpopular?" "*Unpopular?* Be rejected? Well, yes, I am willing. I never faced it before, but I am willing." The next question that came was this: "Would you seek this fullness of the Holy Spirit if it meant *failure* instead of *success*?" That was new light again. I had never thought of such a thing. I had always believed it meant success. But I agreed. I said, "Yes. I choose to be a failure if it be God's will." Last came the third query: "*Are you willing to have no experience?*" "But," I said, "I always thought people who had the baptism of the Spirit had an experience? Did not Finney? Asa Mahan? How am I to know I have had it if I do not get an *experience*?" "Are you willing to walk in bare faith on My word and never have any wonderful experience?" "Yes." These were the three questions the Spirit of God put to me, and then the matter dropped.

A week or two passed, and then God gave some light upon passages of Scripture which led me further on, and gradually brought me into the right attitude for His working. The words struck me: "Thou shalt not *see* wind nor rain, but the valley shall be filled." *"Shall not see!"* Yes, I have agreed to that. I shall see nothing, but the "valley"—my Bible Class—others—*shall be filled.*

Later, I noticed in the story about Elijah and Elisha walking along together, with Elisha longing for the prophet's "mantle": "If thou see *me*, it shall be so." And I understood that I was just to keep my eyes on Christ, and He would see to all the rest. "Yes, Lord, I will keep my eyes right upon Thee."

Afterwards I received more light upon these words: "And they went on and talked." Elijah and Elisha went on together, just talking, and then Elijah was gone! So I am to just go on quietly in communication with the Lord and leave all to Him. He is going to work it all out. I know now that He was just releasing my spirit, getting it into rest and taking all the strain out of it, so that it became quiet and restful. Then there came the morning when I knew that God had answered my prayer. And on this wise—

(1) It was sudden, and when I was not specially thinking about the matter. (2) I knew in my spirit that He had come. (3) My Bible became like a living thing, and was flooded with light. (4) Christ suddenly became to me a real Person. I could not explain how I knew, but He became real to me. (5) When I went

to my Bible Class I found myself able to speak of the Spirit at the back of it, until souls were convicted of sin on every side. (6) Power in prayer, so that it seemed I only needed to ask and have. (7) My spirit took its way to God freed from every fetter that held it to anything on earth.

The floodtide of blessing to souls no words could possibly describe. Next to freedom of utterance so suddenly given, the most striking thing which remains in my memory was a sense (in the spirit) of the intense light of God—not a visible light, but the intensity of the presence of God in such a degree that souls were convicted of sin the instant they entered the room, without one word being spoken to them; and to me, personally, every shade of sin stood out as a black shadow upon the crystal holiness of God, and was seen to be the most horrible thing on earth. How we could *sin* against such a God of holiness and love seemed incredible!

From that time the whole of my work and service was lifted to a different plane, as if it were raised by the incoming of some tidal wave. After liberty of utterance was suddenly given, the outflow of the Spirit swept into the work, and instead of a dead prayer meeting we had prayer meetings so filled with life and freedom of utterance that they were far more attractive than the old popular "social evening." We could spend three hours in prayer with ease, and with effective results. All wanted to pray, and the time was too short for all the "work" that had to be done in the precious prayer time. We had to say that all who wanted to deal with God personally must go to another room, so that the personal should not intervene and hinder the work of prayer for others, locally and in the regions beyond. The floodtide of prayer was soon followed by action, and the praying ones before long were out in the streets seeking to win souls for Christ; for all true overflow from the Holy Spirit must eventually reach the unsaved, just as it did for Pentecost. No influx of the Spirit to a believer will last, or remain in purity from mixture, if it does not flow out in the winning of souls to Christ.

(13) *Power for Aggressive Warfare.*

Not all who receive the enduement of power for witnessing realize that they are called to wage an *aggressive war* upon the invisible hosts of Satan. It is striking to see how the measure of knowlege which the believer has governs the aspect in which the Holy Spirit responds in experience. *Faith is the capacity for receiving*, and faith is exercised up to the extent of knowlege of what faith may take. Faith, too, is often brought about by being placed in a position of *need*. If you think that the enduement of power is for "witnessing" only, that aspect alone will be experienced by you. But if you are plunged into conflict, the very conflict will awaken faith for *victory*.

If the power for service which you receive is so manifested that the kingdom of darkness is affected and greatly shaken, you will know conflict with the powers of darkness. The enemy contests your personal victory all along the line, but not until you know the enduement from on high do you really prove what warfare means. It is when the power of the Holy Spirit comes in *aggressive* warfare that the adversary is touched. The aspect of truth proclaimed also determines the *degree* of conflict. You may witness to the love of God without much opposition from Satan, but if you touch *sin,* or proclaim the cross as the place of death with Christ, or victory over Satan, the enemy is more active in resistance. The message of victory over Satan touches Satan *personally,* and therefore awakens his fiercest resistance.

*   *   *

Finally, the enduement of power for service is for *every* Christian, since every Christian is called to be a witness to Christ. When you ask God for power to witness He looks to see if the "outlet" is ready. Is the *spirit* right? Is the *mind* open to the illumination of the Spirit, or choked up with theories and misconceptions of truth which God cannot endorse by the power of His Spirit? Is the *life* right and all in accord with righteousness? Does the believer *know* right from wrong according to God's standard? For power to witness from the lips includes the witness of the life.

May every believer be willing to be led by the Spirit of God into the fullest surrender to His will, that no cost may be counted too dear to perpetually lay hold of such an enduement of power as will have its outlet in a life of maintained victory and a perpetual warfare on sin and Satan, for the liberation of captive souls to the glory of the Redeemer's name.

SUPPLEMENTARY NOTES

F OR some years I avoided speaking of my
own experience of the baptism of the Holy
Spirit lest others should seek the identically
same experience and thus open the door to
satanic counterfeits, but it has become clear
to me that the personal witness is necessary—safeguarding it with the counsel that
none who read it should expect God to lead
them in exactly the same way, because He
has no rigid system of working with any soul.

* * *

The Holy Spirit, by His incoming, gives
fuller light upon things which may not ap-
pear as sin before. *Known* sin must be put
away in order to receive the Holy Spirit, and
yet, when the will is honestly surrendered,
the Holy Spirit may reveal much deeper
depths yet to be dealt with. This advancing
light and capacity may eventuate in the
enduement for service without *any* definite
asking or seeking for it. Sometimes this may
come about through some special service-
need which compels the believer to cast himself on God for power to accomplish it.

*   *   *

Peter's words in Acts 2:38, spoken to the multitude, show that *in a time when the Holy Spirit is working in great power,* new converts may be regenerated and receive the Holy Spirit at one and the same time! Some say that this is true of every Christian. It *should* be true, if believers were taught as the converts were taught in the early Church; but for Christians today to believe it true in *experience* when actually it is *not* will only render them powerless in their practical life and service. Peter said, as part of his proclamation of the gospel, "and ye shall receive the gift. . . ." It seems, then, that Peter proclaimed the reception of the Holy Spirit as *part of the initial gospel message.* It should be so still, and converts would receive the gift of the Holy Spirit *at conversion* if all the preachers of the gospel today were men endued with the Spirit of God *in the degree that Peter was.* Converts, as a rule, are "born" into the same degree of spiritual life as those who are their spiritual progenitors.

*   *   *

Some dispensational teachers say (1) that the Church which is the Body of Christ was not "born" on the Day of Pentecost, but later, when the apostles so prominent at Pentecost have passed out of sight and Paul comes into view with the "revelation of the Mystery," described by him in Ephesians 3. (2) Others say that the Church had its birth at Pentecost but the miracles ceased as the Jewish dispensation closed. Either of these views may be true or consist of partial truth; I do not wish to debate the points. The danger, however, is *mental* knowledge, which reasons from the letter of the Word and ignores the facts of experience.

The *facts* of experience must be taken into account as throwing light upon the written Word. Those who witness to a baptism of the Spirit in the degree of power for service—such as Finney and others—have been instruments through whom God has reached multitudes of souls.

Unbiased onlookers are compelled to see that any dispensational teaching which eliminates the believer's right to an enduement of power such as the disciples obtained at Pentecost *does not produce the effective results*, either in personal service or church life, which comes from a sought and obtained fullness of the Holy Spirit.

Dispensational truth, when understood in addition to a personal knowledge of the fullness of the Spirit, is of incalculable value—and, we might say, imperatively necessary—for guarding the Spirit-filled believer and for bringing about a proportion of truth which is essential for effective service. The one is the supplement of the other. Paul's *epistles* give the full truth for the Church of Christ, but Paul's *experience* of the baptism of the Spirit (Acts 9:17) is needed to understand and experience the subsequent Spirit-filled life which he *depicted* in his epistles.

Whatever one's view about dispensational teaching, it is a fact that there is no Scriptural ground for asking for "another Pentecost." And it is evident that the degree of the Holy Spirit's working among the believers at Pentecost, in power to witness for Christ, should be the degree for all believers throughout the Christian dispensation.

J.P-L.